DK Kids' First COOK BOOK

Helen Drew
and Angela Wilkes

DK

DORLING KINDERSLEY
www.dk.com

LONDON, NEW YORK, MUNICH,
PARIS, MELBOURNE, DELHI

Editor Jane Elliot
Series Editors Helen Drew and Angela Wilkes
Design Mathewson Bull
Art Director Roger Priddy
Photography Dave King and David Johnson
Illustration Brian Delf
Production Norina Bremner
Managing Editor Jane Yorke
Managing Art Editor Chris Scollen
Home Economists Dolly Meers and Jane Suthering

First published in Great Britain in 1999 by
Dorling Kindersley Limited,
80 Strand, London WC2R 0RL

This edition produced for The Book People Ltd,
Hall Wood Avenue, Haydock, St Helens WA11 9UL

4 6 8 10 9 7 5

A CIP catalogue record for this book
is available from the British Library.
ISBN 0-7513-3995-4

Colour reproduction by Colourscan, Singapore
Printed and bound in China by LEO Paper Products LTD.

Dorling Kindersley would like to thank Michelle Baxter, Dan Bristow,
Jonathan Buckley, Isobel Bulat, Pamela Cowan, Nicola Deschamps,
Mandy Earey, Nancy Graham, Meg Jansz, Pheobe Thoms, and
Henrietta Winthrop for their help in producing this book.

CONTENTS

COOKING BY PICTURES

DK Kids' First Cook Book shows you step-by-step how to make and bake all sorts of delicious things to eat. The easy-to-follow recipes show you which ingredients you need, what to do with them, and what the finished food should look like – life-size! There are lots of great ideas too for creating fun and colourful decorations. Below are the points to look for in each recipe and opposite is an important list of cook's rules to read before you start.

How to use this book

The ingredients
All the ingredients you need for each recipe are shown life-size to help you check you have the right amounts.

Increasing the quantity
Each recipe tells you how many treats the ingredients make. To make more, double or treble the quantities.

Cook's tools
These illustrated checklists show you which utensils you need to have ready before you start cooking.

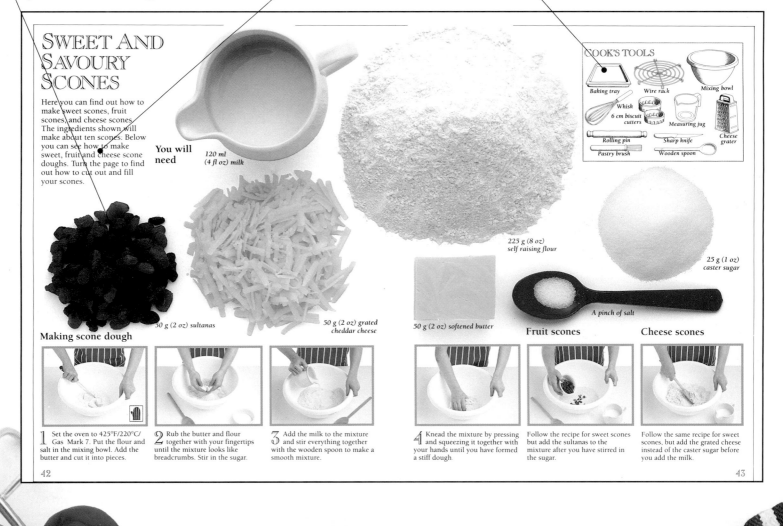

SWEET AND SAVOURY SCONES

Here you can find out how to make sweet scones, fruit scones, and cheese scones. The ingredients shown will make about ten scones. Below you can see how to make sweet, fruit and cheese scone doughs. Turn the page to find out how to cut out and fill your scones.

You will need

120 ml (4 fl oz) milk

225 g (8 oz) self raising flour

25 g (1 oz) caster sugar

50 g (2 oz) sultanas

50 g (2 oz) grated cheddar cheese

50 g (2 oz) softened butter

A pinch of salt

COOK'S TOOLS

Baking tray • Wire rack • Mixing bowl • Whisk • 6 cm biscuit cutters • Measuring jug • Cheese grater • Rolling pin • Sharp knife • Pastry brush • Wooden spoon

Making scone dough

1 Set the oven to 425°F/220°C/ Gas Mark 7. Put the flour and salt in the mixing bowl. Add the butter and cut it into pieces.

2 Rub the butter and flour together with your fingertips until the mixture looks like breadcrumbs. Stir in the sugar.

3 Add the milk to the mixture and stir everything together with the wooden spoon to make a smooth mixture.

4 Knead the mixture by pressing and squeezing it together with your hands until you have formed a stiff dough.

Fruit scones
Follow the recipe for sweet scones but add the sultanas to the mixture after you have stirred in the sugar.

Cheese scones
Follow the same recipe for sweet scones, but add the grated cheese instead of the caster sugar before you add the milk.

42   43

4

Cook's rules

1 Remember you must always have an adult with you before you cook or bake anything.

2 Read each recipe before you start, to make sure you have everything you need.

3 Wash your hands, and put on an apron before you start.

4 Carefully weigh or measure all the ingredients you use.

5 Always wear oven gloves when touching anything hot, or when using the oven.

6 Be careful with sharp knives, and check that saucepan handles are turned away from you so that you do not knock them.

7 If you get burnt, hold the burn under cold running water immediately and call for help.

8 Never leave the kitchen when gas or electric rings are turned on.

9 Always turn the oven off when you have finished with it.

Step-by-step
Step-by-step photographs and easy-to-follow instructions show you what to do at each stage of the recipe.

The oven glove symbol
Whenever you see this symbol in a recipe, always put on oven gloves and ask an adult to help you.

The finished result
The picture at the end of each recipe shows the finished food life-size, and ideas for decoration.

TEATIME TREATS

You can make scones in lots of shapes and sizes. Use different shaped biscuit cutters to make small scones, or make a big scone round with your hands. All scones taste best when they are still warm, either on their own or with butter. For a really special treat, try filling sweet or fruit scones with jam and whipped cream.

COOK'S TOOLS
Small bowl   Whisk
Sharp knife
Knife

Cutting out the scones

1 Grease a baking tray. Gently roll out the dough until it is 2 cm thick. Cut out shapes with biscuit cutters dipped in flour.

2 Put the scones on a baking tray* and brush them with milk. Bake them for 12 to 15 minutes, until firm and risen. Cool them on a wire rack.

A scone round

Whipping the cream

Roll the dough into a circle 2.5 cm thick. Divide the top into eight, then brush it with milk. Bake the round for about 25 minutes.

Whisk the cream in the small bowl until it is thick. Cut the sweet or fruit scones in half and fill them with jam and cream.

You will need

150 ml (¼ pint) double cream

SWEET SCONES

Strawberry jam

Whipped cream

CHEESE SCONES

Jam

A FRUIT SCONE ROUND

Grated cheddar cheese sprinkled on before baking

44

45

*Sprinkle some extra grated cheese on top of the cheese scones.

LITTLE CAKES

Little sponge cakes are simple and quick to make. Here you can see everything you will need to make about ten small and ten tiny plain or cherry cakes. If you wish to make more, you will have to double or treble the amounts of ingredients shown. Don't forget that you will need more icing too!

On the next four pages there are lots of exciting ideas for icing and decorating all your little cakes.

You will need

2 eggs

6 glacé cherries

100 g (4 oz) soft margarine

100 g (4 oz) caster sugar

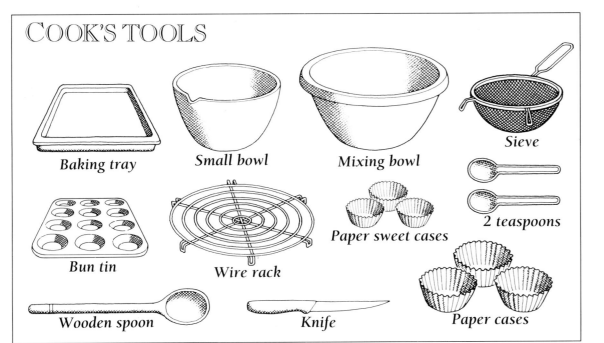

COOK'S TOOLS

Baking tray
Small bowl
Mixing bowl
Sieve

Bun tin
Wire rack
Paper sweet cases
2 teaspoons

Wooden spoon
Knife
Paper cases

What to do

1 Set the oven to 180°C/350°F/ Gas Mark 4. Put the larger paper cases in the bun tin and the sweet cases on the baking tray.

2 Sieve the self-raising flour into the mixing bowl. Add the soft margarine and the caster sugar to the flour.

3 Break the eggs into the bowl. Beat everything together with the wooden spoon until the mixture is soft and creamy.

4 To make cherry cakes, cut the glacé cherries into small pieces with a sharp knife* and stir them into the cake mixture.

5 Put two teaspoonsful of mixture into each larger paper case and one teaspoonful into each sweet case.

6 Bake the tiny cakes for 10 to 15 minutes and the small ones for 20 to 25 minutes. Then put them on a wire rack to cool.

100 g (4 oz) self raising flour

* *Ask an adult to help you.*

7

ICING THE CAKES

You can make lots of different icings for your little cakes. Here you can find out how to make chocolate, white and pink butter icings and how to colour fondant icing and mould it into shapes. Look on the next two pages for lots of decorating ideas.

You will need

100 g (4 oz) soft butter

100 g (4 oz) ready-made fondant icing

2 tablespoons cocoa powder

3 drops red food colouring

215 g (7¹/₂ oz) icing sugar

COOK'S TOOLS

Mixing bowl   Small bowl

Wooden spoon

Sharp knife

Sieve   Knife

What to do

1 Put half the butter into the mixing bowl and cut it into small pieces. Beat it with the wooden spoon until it is creamy.

2 Sift 125 g (4 oz) of icing sugar into a small bowl. Mix the sugar into the butter a little at a time until the icing is creamy.

3 Divide the icing in half. Put half of it in a small bowl. Beat the red colouring into the other half to make pink icing.

Fondant icing

4 To make chocolate icing, use 90 g (3½ oz) of icing sugar and the cocoa powder and follow steps 1 and 2 above.

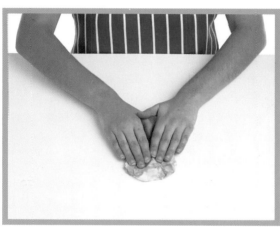

1 To make pink fondant icing, add 3 drops of red colouring to the fondant. Knead it until the colour is even.

2 Make a roll of fondant for the elephant's trunk and shape flat circles for its ears. Make pig's ears from flat ovals of fondant.

Cakes with faces

1 Remove the cakes from their cases. Arrange the small and tiny cakes together to make faces with ears or noses or both.

2 Ice the bottom and sides of a tiny cake and stick it on top of a small cake covered with the same coloured icing.

3 When you have iced all your cakes, give them faces by decorating them with sweets and chocolates before the icing dries.

FUNNY FACES

Little cakes are great fun to make and they look really bright and colourful as well. You will need to look out for all sorts of different chocolates and sweets to use for decoration. Copy the butterflies, soldier, teddy bear, elephant and other funny face cakes shown here or experiment with some ideas of your own!

Why not try making funny face cakes that look like your family and pets for a special family meal or party.

You will need

Liquorice stumps

Red liquorice laces

Liquorice strips

White chocolate drops

Chocolate drops

Glacé cherries

White chocolate buttons

Chocolate buttons

Coloured chocolate sweets

Chocolate sugar strands

CHERRY CAKES

Eat your cherry cakes as they are, or iced and decorated with sweets.

Pieces of glacé cherry

BUTTERFLIES

Sponge wings

Butter icing

Cut a circle out of some small cakes and then cut the circles in half to make wings. Fill the hole in the cakes with butter icing and put a wing on either side.

PIG

Chocolate drop eyes

Pink fondant ears

Chocolate drop nostrils

Red sweet tongue

TEDDY BEAR

Tiny cake cut in half with pieces of chocolate buttons for ears

Yellow sweet and chocolate drop eyes

Red sweet nose

Chocolate sugar strand snout

SEAL

Chocolate drop and white chocolate button eyes

Liquorice whiskers

RACOON

Chocolate sugar strand fur

White chocolate button and liquorice nose

Chocolate button ears

White chocolate drop and liquorice eyes

DOG

Chocolate drop eyes

Liquorice nose

Chocolate sugar strand whiskers

Red sweet tongue

SOLDIER

Chocolate sugar strand busby

Red liquorice eyebrows

Chocolate drop and yellow sweet eyes

Glacé cherry nose

Red liquorice mouth

Liquorice chinstrap and moustache

ELEPHANT

Pink fondant circles on tiny cakes for ears

Red sweet

White chocolate drop tusks

Chocolate drop eyes

Pink fondant trunk curled up on a tiny cake

Surprise Cake

For birthdays, parties and other celebrations it is nice to make a special cake.
Here is a recipe for a delicious and light sponge cake that you can decorate however you like. You can find out how to make the cake below, and then turn to the next two pages to see how to ice and decorate it.

You will need

150 g (6 oz) softened butter

150 g (6 oz) plain flour

Making the cake

1 Set the oven at 180°C/350°F/ Gas Mark 4. Rub some butter around the insides of the two sandwich tins thoroughly.

2 Put the softened butter and sugar in the mixing bowl. Beat them with the wooden spoon until the mixture is pale and creamy.

3 Beat the eggs in a small bowl. Add them to the butter and sugar mixture a little at a time stirring it in well until it is smooth.

12

3 eggs

150 g (6 oz) caster sugar

COOK'S TOOLS

Mixing bowl

Fork

Wooden spoon

2 20-cm (8-inch)
Sandwich cake tins

Small bowl

Wire rack

1½ teaspoons baking powder

4 Sift the flour and baking powder into the mixture and mix well. The cake mixture should be soft and light.

5 Pour half of the cake mixture into each sandwich tin and smooth it level. Place the tins in the oven for 20 to 25 minutes.

6 The cakes are done when well-risen and brown. They should feel springy in the middle. Turn them out on to a wire rack to cool.

Now turn the page.

EASTER CAKE

This cake is filled and topped with chocolate butter icing and decorated. Copy the Easter Cake, or make up a new picture.

You will need

COOK'S TOOLS

Sieve

Mixing bowl

Knife

Wooden spoon

15–30 ml (1–2 tablespoons) milk

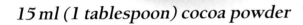

15 ml (1 tablespoon) cocoa powder

75 g (3 oz) softened butter

150 g (6 oz) icing sugar

Icing the cake

1 Put the butter in the bowl and cut it into small pieces. Beat it hard with the wooden spoon until it is soft and creamy.

2 Sift the icing sugar and cocoa powder into the bowl, a little at a time, mixing them in with the butter. Then stir in the milk.

3 When the cakes are cool, spread half the icing on one of them. Put the other cake on top and spread the rest of the icing over it.

Arranging the Easter Cake

4 Now decorate the cake. Press the sweets firmly into the icing. Start with the border, do the nest and arrange the hen last of all.

Blanched almonds

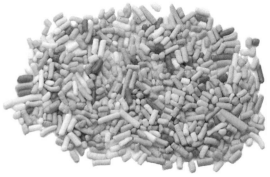

Sugar strands

Coloured chocolate sweets

Chocolate drops

The finished cake

Almond beak

Almond tail

Chocolate drops

Brown sweet border

Sugar strands

Coloured chocolate sweets

15

A RICH CHOCOLATE CAKE

No birthday or party is complete without a surprise cake – so here's how to make a wonderful chocolate cake that tastes delicious. Look on the next four pages to find out how to cut up, ice and decorate the cake to make an amazing chocolate dinosaur that you will never forget!

You will need

100 g (4 oz) softened butter

250 ml (8 fl oz) milk

2 large eggs

1 tablespoon lemon juice

COOK'S TOOLS

Wire rack

Mixing bowl

Greaseproof paper

Greased 22 cm deep cake tin

Pencil

Scissors

Measuring jug

Dessert spoon

Sieve

Wooden spoon

What to do

1 Set the oven to 180°C/350°F/ Gas Mark 4. Draw round the cake tin on greaseproof paper. Cut out the circle and put it in the tin.

2 Stir the lemon juice into the milk. Put the butter and half the sugar into the mixing bowl and beat it until pale and fluffy.

16

250 g (9 oz)
caster sugar

1 teaspoon bicarbonate
of soda

50g (2 oz)
cocoa powder

225 g (8 oz) plain flour

3 Beat the eggs into the mixture one at a time. Stir in the rest of the sugar. Sift the flour, soda and cocoa powder together.

4 Beat in half the milk and fold in half the flour. Add the rest of the milk and then the rest of the flour. Mix until smooth.

5 Pour the mixture into the cake tin and bake it for one hour. Then tip the cake out of the tin and leave it on a wire rack to cool.

Cutting the Cake

Cut the cake into the pieces shown below with a sharp knife*. Be very careful to make your cuts in the right places. If you make a mistake, stick the cake back together with some of the butter icing shown over the page and start again. Opposite, you can see how to make marzipan scales and spikes for the dinosaur. If you don't like marzipan, use 225 g (8 oz) of the fondant icing shown on page 8 instead.

Body

Leg   Leg

Spare pieces of cake that you can eat now!

Tail

Head

Neck

18

Ask an adult to help you with this.

You will need

2 tablespoons
beaten egg

100 g (4 oz) ground almonds

¹/4 teaspoon green food colouring

100 g (4 oz) icing sugar

Making marzipan

Put the sugar and almonds in the mixing bowl and stir them together. Add the egg and mix to form a firm paste.

Marzipan scales

Divide the marzipan in half and knead the green colouring into one half. Roll it into balls and squash them flat.

Marzipan spikes

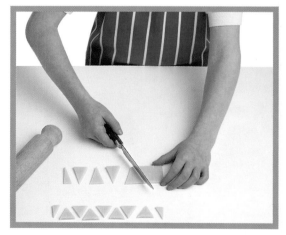

Roll out the plain marzipan until it is 3 mm thick. Cut out* twelve small and six big spikes. Mark a line down the middle of each one.

A DELICIOUS DINOSAUR

And here is the finished dinosaur!
Find out how to make green
butter icing on pages 8 to 9.
You will need to treble the
ingredients shown and add
a few drops of green food colouring.

You will need

1 white chocolate
button   1 chocolate drop

Marzipan spikes (see page 19)

Marzipan scales (see page 19)

White chocolate drops

Green butter icing
(See pages 8-9)

Large marzipan spikes

Marzipan scales

White chocolate drop claws

Decorating the cake

1 Put the cake on the board you will be serving it on. Turn the head on its side and then cut out the dinosaur's jaw.

2 Use half of the icing to ice the top and sides of each section of the dinosaur. Stick the sections together with more icing.

3 Smooth the rest of the icing over the whole cake. Decorate the cake with marzipan shapes and chocolate drops, as shown.

The finished cake

Small marzipan spikes

Eye made of a white chocolate button with a chocolate drop on top

White chocolate drop teeth

Green marzipan scale

21

QUICK BREAD

Making bread is great fun. This recipe makes enough dough for eight rolls. Here you can see how to make the dough. The next two pages show you how to make and decorate the rolls.

You will need

3 g (½ sachet) quick-action dried yeast

1 dessertspoon vegetable or sunflower oil

A large pinch of salt

COOK'S TOOLS

Mixing bowl

Measuring jug

Kitchen scissors

Pastry brush

Wooden spoon

Greased baking tray

Wire rack

Making the dough

210 ml (⅜ pint) warm water

350 g (12 oz)
strong white flour

1 Set the oven to 230°C/450°F/ Gas Mark 8. Put the flour, yeast and salt in the mixing bowl. Add the vegetable oil and water.

2 Mix everything together into a firm dough. If the dough is sticky, add a little flour. Add a little water if it is too dry.

3 Put the dough on a floured table. Knead the dough by pushing, folding and turning it for 5 minutes.

4 Shape the dough into rolls (see next page). Put them on to the greased baking tray. Then put them in a warm place*.

5 When the rolls have doubled in size, then you can decorate them however you want (see the next page).

6 Bake them for 15 to 20 minutes. They are done if they sound hollow when tapped underneath. Put them on the wire rack to cool.

Ask an adult for a suitable, warm place. 23

TWIST AND ROLL

You can make bread rolls in all sorts of different shapes. You can vary them even more by using different seeds to make crunchy toppings.

To make the rolls, break the bread dough into eight pieces, all about the same size, then follow the instructions on the right. Remember that the baked rolls will be twice as big as the dough, because they will grow when rising.

TORTOISE ROLL

Stick tiny balls of dough around a roll to look like four legs, a head and a tail. Mark the top of the roll to look like a shell.

PRICKLY HEDGEHOG

Make a pointed snout shape at one end of a roll. Snip the rest of the roll, the hedgehog's body, with scissors to make prickles.

Decorating the rolls

When the rolls have risen and are ready to bake, you can decorate them with any of the things shown below. To give the rolls a golden brown glaze, you will also need a beaten egg and a pastry brush.

You will need

Sesame seeds

Caraway seeds

1 beaten egg

Flower roll sprinkled with caraway seeds

Poppy seeds

Currants

Prickly hedgehog with currant eyes and nose

Brush the rolls lightly with the beaten egg. Sprinkle seeds over them and press them gently into place. The rolls are now ready to go into the oven (see the previous page).

Cottage roll sprinkled with poppy seeds

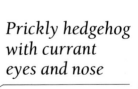

COTTAGE ROLL

Make a smaller ball of dough than the others. Brush the base of it with water. Stick it to a larger roll and make a dent in the top.

SNAIL ROLL

Roll a ball of dough into a sausage shape. Brush one side of it with water and wind it into a coil, leaving one end as the head.

FLOWER ROLL

Flatten a ball of dough slightly. Snip all round the edge of the dough with kitchen scissors to make petal shapes.

The finished rolls on a cooling rack

25

FRUITY BREAD

A Christmas wreath not only tastes good; it looks really festive too! Here you can see all you need to make a fruity bread wreath. The wreath will rise more quickly if you put it in an oiled plastic bag and then leave it in a warm place. Turn the page to see how to make the icing and marzipan decoration for your wreath.

You will need

25 g (1 oz) butter

1 small egg

75 ml (3 fl oz) warm milk

½ teaspoon salt

25 g (1 oz) soft brown sugar

225 g (8 oz) strong white flour

1 Set oven to 200°C/400°F/Gas Mark 6. Put the sugar, flour, yeast, salt, spice and cinnamon in the bowl and stir them together.

2 Add the butter and cut it up. Rub everything together with your fingertips until the mixture looks like fine breadcrumbs.

3 Add the fruit, egg and milk. Mix them together to make a ball of dough. Knead the dough on a floured surface for five minutes.

1 sachet easy blend yeast

COOK'S TOOLS

Pastry brush

Greased baking tray

Mixing bowl

Wire rack

Knife

Wooden spoon

Measuring jug

Palette knife

15 g (1/2 oz) mixed peel

1/2 teaspoon ground mixed spice

1 teaspoon ground cinnamon

40 g (1 1/2 oz) currants

4 Roll the dough into two sausages about 60 cm long. Put the sausages side by side and twist them together.

5 Bend the twist into a ring on the baking tray. Wet the ends of the twist with water and stick them together.

6 Leave the ring in a warm place until it has doubled in size. Bake it for 20 to 25 minutes, then move it on to a wire rack, to cool.

A Christmas Wreath

Turn your fruity wreath into a Christmas treat with a tangy lemon icing and some marzipan leaves and berries. You can find out how to make marzipan on page 19, but if you prefer, you can use ready-made marzipan or the fondant icing used on page 8.

25 g (1 oz) marzipan (for holly leaves)

15 g (½ oz) marzipan (for holly berries)

1 tablespoon lemon juice

You will need

12 drops of green food colouring

12 drops of red food colouring

175 g (6 oz) icing sugar

Colouring marzipan

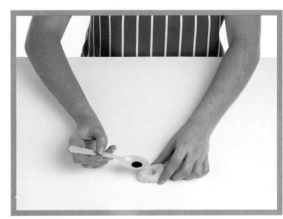

Make a hole with your finger in the marzipan and add the food colouring. Knead the marzipan until it is an even colour.

Holly leaves

Roll the green marzipan out on a sugared surface until it is 3mm thick. Cut out leaves with the cutter (or a knife).

Holly berries

Take small pieces of red marzipan and roll them into balls with your fingers. Try to keep all the balls the same size.

Making icing

COOK'S TOOLS

Small bowl

Sieve

Small holly leaf cutters*

Rolling pin

Wooden spoon

1 Sift the icing sugar into the small bowl. Add the lemon juice and stir with the wooden spoon until the icing is smooth.

2 Spoon the icing along the top of the wreath and let it drip down the sides. Decorate the wreath before the icing sets.

The finished Christmas wreath

Marzipan holly leaves

Marzipan holly berries

Serve the ring cut into wedges with some berries and leaves on each wedge.

Snowy white icing

* Use a knife if you can't find any cutters.

SPEEDY PIZZA

This pizza is quick and easy to make. Here you can see how to make the pizza and sauce, and on the next page are some ideas for toppings. You can make two 10 cm (4 in) pizzas from the ingredients below.

You will need for the pizza

A pinch of salt

40 g (1½ oz) butter

3–4 tablespoons milk

150 g (6 oz) self-raising flour

50 g (2 oz) grated cheese

COOK'S TOOLS

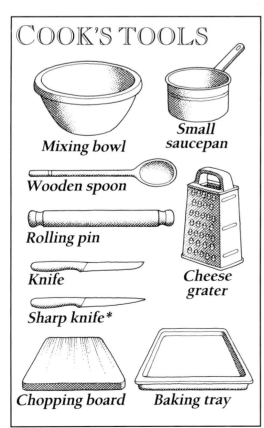

Mixing bowl

Small saucepan

Wooden spoon

Rolling pin

Cheese grater

Knife

Sharp knife*

Chopping board

Baking tray

For the sauce

1 small onion

1 dessertspoon tomato purée

A pinch each of salt and pepper

1 small tin tomatoes

*Make sure that an adult helps you when you are using a sharp knife.

Making the sauce

1 Set the oven at 220°C/425°F/ Gas Mark 7. Peel the onion, then cut it in half and chop it up finely on the chopping board.

2 Put the chopped onion in the saucepan. Add the tomatoes, tomato purée, the salt and pepper and stir the mixture together.

3 Cook the mixture over a low heat for about 15 minutes, stirring from time to time. Then turn off the heat and let it cool.

Making the dough

1 While the sauce is cooking, make the dough. Put the flour, salt and butter in the mixing bowl. Cut the butter into small pieces.

2 Rub the pieces of butter into the flour between your fingertips and thumbs until the mixture looks like breadcrumbs.

3 Add the grated cheese and milk to the flour mixture. Mix everything together until you have a smooth ball of dough.

4 Divide the dough in two and make each into a ball. Roll each ball of dough into a circular shape about 10 cm (4 in) across.

5 Lay the circles of dough on the greased baking tray. Spoon the tomato sauce on to them, spreading it out evenly to the edges.

6 Decorate the pizzas (see next page). Put them in the oven to cook for 15–20 minutes, until the edges are golden brown.

Now turn the page.

PARTY PIZZAS

Once you have made the basic pizzas, you can turn them into picture pizzas, using any of the ingredients below, before cooking them. Try making one of the pizzas shown here, or experiment with ideas of your own.

Sliced ham cut into strips

Grated cheese

Topping ingredients

Stoned black olives

Sliced peppers

Cheese sliced then cut into shapes

Sliced cooked sausage

ITALIAN PIZZA

Chopped red pepper

Sliced cooked sausage

Chopped ham

Sliced mushrooms

Sweetcorn

Sliced mushroom

Tinned sweetcorn

Grated cheese

Chopped green pepper

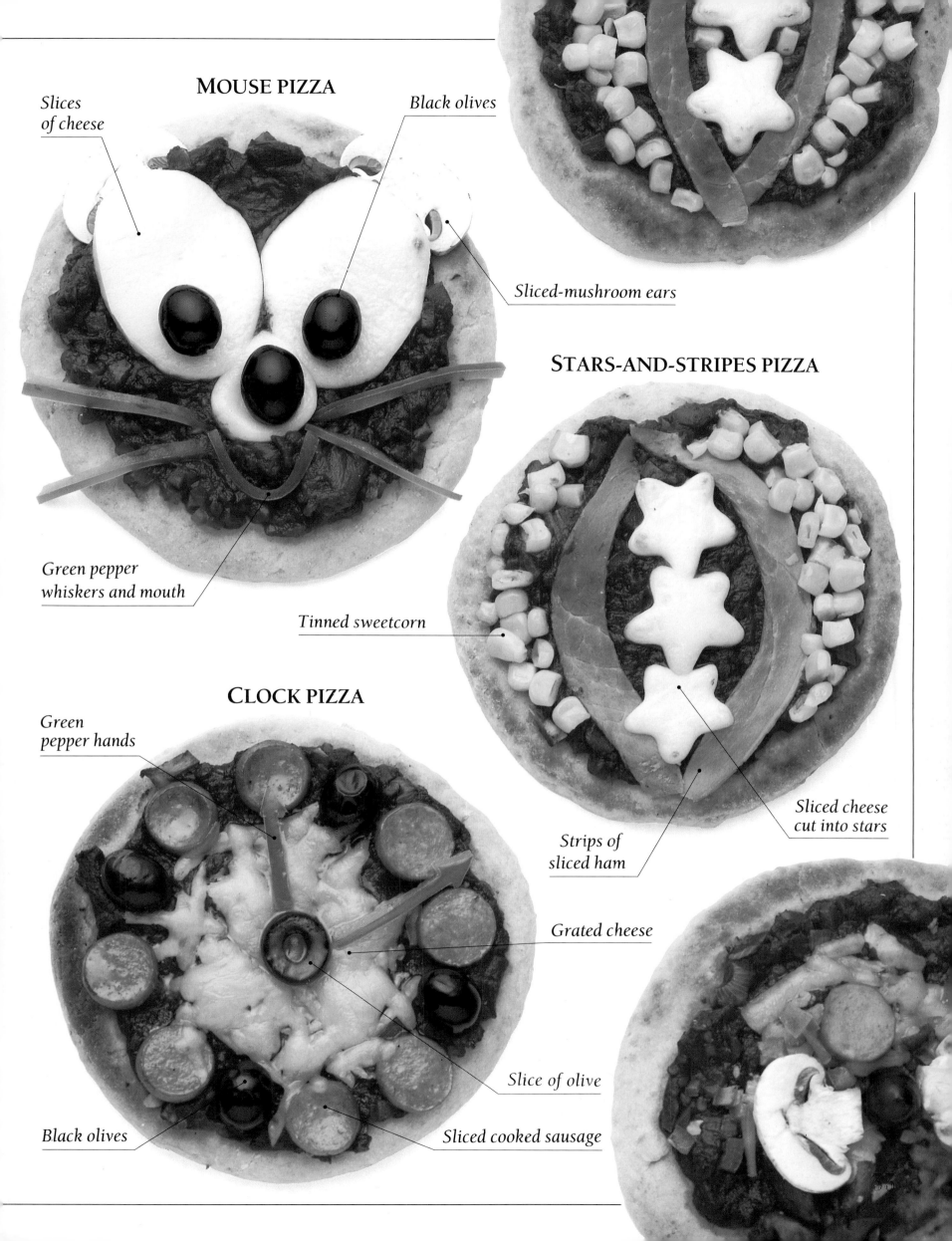

MOUSE PIZZA

Slices
of cheese

Black olives

Sliced-mushroom ears

Green pepper
whiskers and mouth

STARS-AND-STRIPES PIZZA

Tinned sweetcorn

CLOCK PIZZA

Green
pepper hands

Grated cheese

Slice of olive

Black olives

Sliced cooked sausage

Sliced cheese
cut into stars

Strips of
sliced ham

CHEESY POTATO BOATS

Stuffed potatoes are a meal in themselves and are easy to make. Here are some unusual ideas on how to decorate them once you have cooked them. Potatoes take a long time to cook, so put them in the oven 1 to 1½ hours before you want to eat them*.

For two people you will need

2 knobs of butter

50 g (2 oz) grated cheese

1 large scrubbed potato

For decoration you can use any of these things

Button mushrooms

Strips of cucumber

Stoned black olives

Carrots, sliced or cut into sticks

Sliced cheese cut into shapes

COOK'S TOOLS

Small bowl

Knife

Fork

Tablespoon

Cheese grater

Greased baking tray

Sliced peppers, cut into strips

Shredded lettuce

Watercress

* Ask an adult to check if the potatoes are cooked. Leave the oven on for step 3.

Cooking the potatoes

1 Set the oven at 200°C/400°F/ Gas Mark 6. Prick the potatoes and place them on the greased baking tray. Bake for 1¼ hours*.

2 When cooked, cut the potatoes in half lengthways. Scoop out the middles into the bowl and mash them. Stir in the butter and cheese.

3 Spoon the mixture back into the potato skins and level them off. Then put them back into the oven for another 15 minutes.

*Carefully prick the potatoes using a fork or skewer.

Decorating the potatoes

You can decorate the potatoes once they have been cooked for a second time. Make them into sailing boats, steamer ships or rowing boats as shown here.

SAILING JACKET

Yellow pepper flag

Cocktail-stick mast

Cheese sail

Red pepper deck

POTATO ROWING BOAT

Black olives

Carrot oars

Watercress leaves

Cucumber oars

Black olives

Shredded lettuce for sea

STUFFED STEAMER

Watercress steam

Funnels made of sliced carrot and mushroom stalks

Red pepper

35

PERFECT PASTRY

Here and on the next five pages you can find out how to make tiny fruit tarts and savoury quiches. These two pages show you how to make the pastry cases. These quantities will make about thirty small tarts, depending on the size of the tins you use.

You will need

25 g (1 oz) caster sugar
(for sweet tarts only)

About 3 tablespoons water

100 g (4 oz) margarine or butter

A pinch of salt

COOK'S TOOLS

Mixing bowl

Knife

Fork

Rolling pin

Wooden spoon

Pastry
cutter

Patty tin or
little tartlet tins

Wire rack

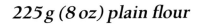

225 g (8 oz) plain flour

Making the pastry

1 Turn the oven on to 200°C/
400°F/Gas Mark 6. Put the
flour, butter and salt in the mixing
bowl. Cut up the butter.

2 Rub the flour and butter
together with your fingertips
until they look like breadcrumbs.
For sweet tarts, add the sugar.

3 Now mix in the water, a little
at a time. You should have a
soft ball of dough that leaves the
sides of the bowl clean.

4 Sprinkle flour on to the table
and your rolling pin. Put the
dough on to the table and roll it
out until it is quite thin.

5 Stamp circles out of the pastry,
using a pastry-cutter or cup.
The circles should be a bit bigger
than your tart tins.

6 Lay each circle of pastry over a
tin. Gather in the edges and
press the pastry into place so that
it fits the tin.

For sweet tarts

7 Prick the bases of the pastry
cases with a fork. Put them in
the oven and bake them for 15
minutes, until golden brown.

8 Let the tins cool, then lever the
pastry cases out with a knife
and put them on to a wire rack.
See how to fill them over the page.

For savoury tarts

9 Add the filling now (see pages
40–41). Then put the tarts in
the oven to bake for about 20
minutes, until the filling sets.

Turn to the next four pages for filling ideas. 37

Fruit Tarts

To make these fruit tarts, cook the pastry cases first (see the previous page). Then fill them with fruit and glaze them with melted jam. It is best to use soft fruits like those shown below, because you don't have to cook them.

You will need

450 g (1 lb) fruit, such as:

Tinned or fresh pineapple

Cooked, sweet pastry cases

Raspberries

Blackberries

Seedless grapes

COOK'S TOOLS

Wooden spoon

Small saucepan

Sharp knife

Pastry brush

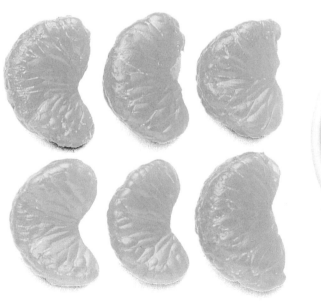

Tinned mandarin oranges

100 g (4 oz) redcurrant jelly (or sieved apricot jam)

38

Filling the tarts

 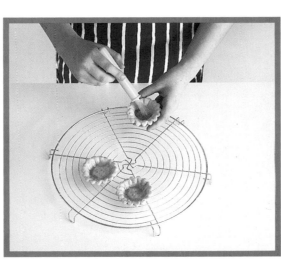 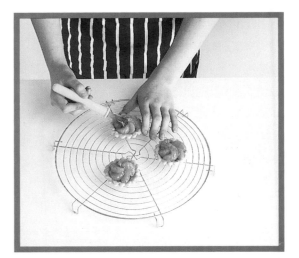

1 Make a glaze for the tarts by melting the redcurrant jelly or sieved apricot jam in the small saucepan over a low heat.

2 Brush the insides of the pastry cases with the glaze. Wash the fresh fruit and drain the tinned fruit. Cut the grapes in half.

3 Arrange the fruit in the pastry cases, as shown below. Then brush the fruit with the glaze, which will set as it cools.

The finished tarts

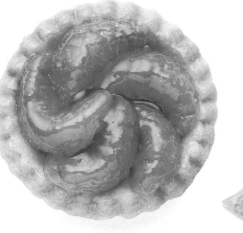

This tart has a ring of blackberries with a raspberry in the centre.

Arrange mandarin orange segments so they overlap to form a circle.

Use slices of grape, four pineapple segments and a grape for the centre.

Use pineapple, mandarin segments, raspberries and halved grapes.

The grape in the centre of this is put between two chunks of pineapple.

This one has mandarin orange segments and blackberries.

MINI QUICHES

When making quiches or savoury tarts, put the filling in the pastry cases before you cook them. You can add whatever you want to the basic filling of eggs and milk to give the quiches any flavour you like. Try combinations of the filling ingredients shown below.

You will need

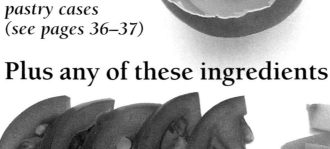

2 eggs

Uncooked, unsweetened pastry cases (see pages 36–37)

200 ml (⅓ pt) milk

Chopped spring onions

Plus any of these ingredients

Sliced tomatoes

Strips of sliced ham

Finely sliced leeks

Sliced mushrooms

Grated cheese

Tinned tuna fish

What you do

1 Slice the tomatoes and mushrooms. Chop the ham and spring onion. Drain the tuna and sweetcorn. Grate the cheese.

2 Break the eggs into the measuring jug. Beat them well with the fork. Pour in the milk and whisk the mixture together.

3 Arrange the fillings in the pastry cases, pour on the egg mixture. Put them in the oven for 20 minutes (see page 37).

The finished quiches

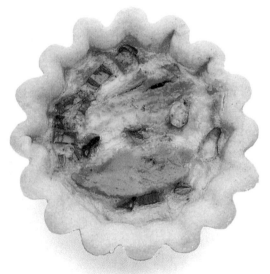

This quiche is filled with a mixture of tuna fish and spring onion.

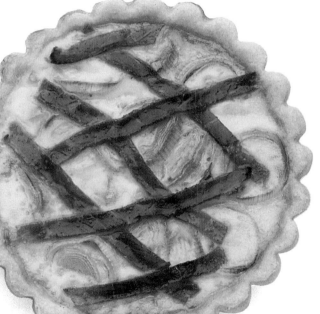

Place sliced leeks in this quiche. Then put strips of ham on top.

Tinned tuna fish and sliced tomatoes are used in this quiche.

This quiche has grated cheese topped with sliced tomatoes.

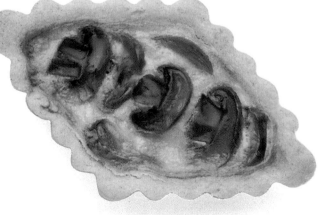

In this quiche sliced mushrooms are arranged to overlap slightly.

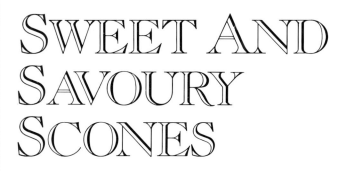

SWEET AND SAVOURY SCONES

Here you can find out how to make sweet scones, fruit scones, and cheese scones. The ingredients shown will make about ten scones. Below you can see how to make sweet, fruit and cheese scone doughs. Turn the page to find out how to cut out and fill your scones.

You will need

120 ml (4 fl oz) milk

50 g (2 oz) sultanas

50 g (2 oz) grated cheddar cheese

Making scone dough

1 Set the oven to 425°F/220°C/ Gas Mark 7. Put the flour and salt in the mixing bowl. Add the butter and cut it into pieces.

2 Rub the butter and flour together with your fingertips until the mixture looks like breadcrumbs. Stir in the sugar.

3 Add the milk to the mixture and stir everything together with the wooden spoon to make a smooth mixture.

225 g (8 oz) self raising flour

25 g (1 oz) caster sugar

A pinch of salt

50 g (2 oz) softened butter

Fruit scones

Cheese scones

4 Knead the mixture by pressing and squeezing it together with your hands until you have formed a stiff dough.

Follow the recipe for sweet scones but add the sultanas to the mixture after you have stirred in the sugar.

Follow the same recipe for sweet scones, but add the grated cheese instead of the caster sugar before you add the milk.

43

TEATIME TREATS

You can make scones in lots of shapes and sizes. Use different shaped biscuit cutters to make small scones, or make a big scone round with your hands. All scones taste best when they are still warm, either on their own or with butter. For a really special treat, try filling sweet or fruit scones with jam and whipped cream.

COOK'S TOOLS

Small bowl

Whisk

Sharp knife

Knife

You will need

Jam

Cutting out the scones

1 Grease a baking tray. Gently roll out the dough until it is 2 cm thick. Cut out shapes with biscuit cutters dipped in flour.

2 Put the scones on a baking tray* and brush them with milk. Bake them for 12 to 15 minutes, until firm and risen. Cool them on a wire rack.

A scone round

Roll the dough into a circle 2.5 cm thick. Divide the top into eight, then brush it with milk. Bake the round for about 25 minutes.

Whipping the cream

Whisk the cream in the small bowl until it is thick. Cut the sweet or fruit scones in half and fill them with jam and cream.

Sprinkle some extra grated cheese on top of the cheese scones.

150 ml (¹/4 pint)
double cream

Strawberry
jam

Whipped cream

CHEESE SCONES

A FRUIT
SCONE ROUND

Grated cheddar cheese
sprinkled on before baking

45

SIMPLE SHORTBREAD

Two-tone shortbread biscuits are great fun to make and eat. On this page you can see everything you will need to make plain and chocolate shortbread dough. The ingredients shown below make enough shortbread for eight owl's eyes, eight lollipops and twelve window biscuits. Look on the next page to find out how to make each biscuit and to see the finished results.

For plain shortbread

You will need

125 g (4 oz) softened butter

50 g (2 oz) caster sugar

15 g (¹/2 oz) cocoa powder

COOK'S TOOLS

Pastry brush

Knife

Rolling pin

Wooden spoon

Palette knife

2 greased baking trays

Wire rack

Lollipop sticks

Mixing bowl

Sieve

blanched almonds

175 g (6 oz) plain flour

For chocolate shortbread

125 g (4 oz) softened butter

50 g (2 oz) caster sugar

160 g (5 1/2 oz) plain flour

Making plain shortbread

3 tablespoons milk

1 Set the oven to 350°F/180°C/ Gas Mark 4. Sieve 175 g (6 oz) flour into the mixing bowl. Stir in 50 g (2 oz) of sugar.

2 Add 125 g (4 oz) butter, cut up. Rub the flour, sugar and butter together with your fingers until the mixture is like breadcrumbs.

3 Add a tablespoonful of milk to the mixture. Mix everything together with your hands to form a ball of dough.

Making chocolate shortbread

1 Sift 160 g (5 1/2 oz) flour and the cocoa powder together. Make the chocolate dough in the same way as the plain dough.

2 Divide each ball of dough into three equal pieces. You will need one plain and one chocolate piece to make each type of biscuit.

BISCUIT BAZAAR

Owl's eyes

1 Roll a piece of each type of dough into a square 15 cm by 15 cm. Brush the top of each square with milk.

2 Put one square on top of another and roll them up together. Then cut the roll into 16 slices, as shown.

3 Stick two slices together with milk to make each biscuit. Put the biscuits on a baking tray. Add an almond beak to each one.

Lollipops

1 Roll out the chocolate dough into a square 10 cm by 10 cm. Make the plain dough into a roll 10 cm long with your hands.

2 Brush the chocolate square with milk and wrap it round the plain roll. Squeeze the ends of the chocolate dough together.

3 Cut the roll into eight slices. Put the slices on to the baking tray and push a lollipop stick into the middle of each one.

Windows

1 Shape the two sorts of dough into rectangles 4 cm by 9 cm with your hands. Cut them in half lengthways.

2 Stick two strips of plain and chocolate dough together with milk. Stick the other two strips on top of them, as shown.

3 Cut the block of dough strips into 12 square slices with a sharp knife. Put the slices on to a baking tray.

Cooking the biscuits

4 Bake the biscuits in the top half of the oven for 15 to 20 minutes until they are a pale gold colour. The lollipop biscuits are thicker and will take slightly longer to cook.

When the biscuits are done, carefully move them from the baking trays and put on a wire rack to cool and harden.

Storing your biscuits

Biscuits go soggy if they are left out for too long. Store them in an airtight tin or jar to keep them fresh and crunchy.

The finished biscuits

OWL'S EYES

LOLLIPOPS

WINDOWS

Puff Pastry

You can make lots of mouth-watering pastries with ready-made puff pastry. Here you can find out how to make Eccles cakes, palmiers (palm tree-shaped pastries) and cheese twists.

The ingredients shown are enough to make about thirty pastries. Turn the page to see the finished results.

You will need

1 egg

50 g (2 oz) demerara sugar (for palmiers)

¹/₂ teaspoon caster sugar (for Eccles cakes)

¹/₄ teaspoon ground nutmeg (for Eccles cakes)

15 g (¹/₂ oz) soft butter (for Eccles cakes)

350 g (12 oz) ready-made puff pastry

15 g (¹/₂ oz) demerara sugar (for Eccles cakes)

15 g (¹/₂ oz) mixed peel (for Eccles cakes)

COOK'S TOOLS

Measuring jug   Baking tray   Small bowl

10 cm plain biscuit cutters

Wire rack

Rolling pin

Wooden spoon   Fork

Knife   Pastry brush

25 g
(1 oz)
*chopped
roasted hazelnuts
(for palmiers)*

*50 g (2 oz) grated cheddar cheese
(for cheese twists)*

*40 g (1½ oz) currants
(for Eccles cakes)*

What to do

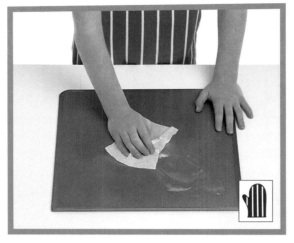

1 Set the oven to 220°C/425°F/
Gas Mark 7. Grease a baking
tray with some butter. Beat the egg
in a jug with a fork.

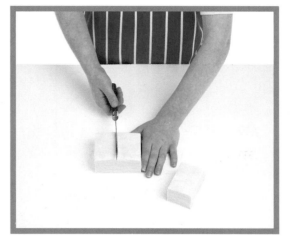

2 Put the pastry on a floured
surface and divide it into
three equal pieces. You will need
one piece of pastry for each recipe.

Eccles cakes

1 Roll out the pastry on a
floured surface until it is 3 mm
thick. Cut out six circles with the
plain biscuit cutter.

2 Put the currants, peel, butter,
15 g (½ oz) demerara sugar,
and nutmeg in a small bowl and
mix them together.

3 Put a teaspoon of mixture in
the centre of each circle. Brush
the circles with egg and pinch the
edges together.

4 Turn the parcels over and
press them flat. Cut two slits
in the top. Brush them with egg
and sprinkle caster sugar on top.

Pastries On Parade

Hazelnut palmiers

1 Roll out the pastry into a rectangle 30 cm by 20 cm. Brush it with egg and sprinkle on two thirds of the sugar and nuts.

2 Fold the short sides of the rectangle into the middle. Brush them with egg and sprinkle with the rest of the sugar and nuts.

3 Fold the folded edges into the middle. Brush the top with egg. Fold the pastry in half to form a roll. Cut it into 16 slices.

Cheese twists

1 Roll out the pastry into a rectangle 25 cm by 20 cm. Brush it with egg. Sprinkle the cheese over half of the rectangle.

2 Fold the pastry over the cheese to make a sandwich and roll it flat. Trim the edges with a knife. Brush the sandwich with egg.

3 Cut the sandwich lengthways into 20 strips. Twist each strip several times and press the ends on to the baking tray.

Baking the pastries

Bake the pastries on a greased baking tray. Cheese twists and palmiers should be baked for 10 minutes and the Eccles cakes for 15 minutes. The pastries are ready when they are crisp and golden brown. Once they are cooked, take the pastries out of the oven and put them on a wire rack to cool. Pastries taste best on the day they are made, so you can eat them as soon as they are cool!

The finished pastries

ECCLES CAKES

HAZELNUT PALMIERS

CHEESE TWISTS

PASTRY IN A PAN

Choux pastry* is great fun to make as it puffs up to two or three times its size when you bake it. Here and on the next five pages, you can find out how to make and decorate lots of different choux cakes. The ingredients shown below will make about five spiders, snakes, puffs and éclairs, and lots of worms.

You will need

3/4 teaspoon salt

100 g (3½ oz) butter

150 g (5 oz) plain flour

4 eggs

250 ml (8 fl oz) water

1 beaten egg

COOK'S TOOLS

Wooden board   Small bowl   Sieve   Saucepan   Measuring jug

Baking tray   Piping bags with sizes 0, 2, 6 and 8 plain nozzles   Wire rack   Cocktail sticks

Fork   Pastry brush   Wooden spoon

* Choux is French for puff.

What to do

1 Set the oven to 200°C/400°F/ Gas Mark 6. Grease the baking tray. Sieve the flour into the small bowl.

2 Put the water, salt and butter into the pan and heat them gently until the butter has melted and the mixture begins to bubble.

3 Remove the saucepan from the heat and stand it on a wooden board. Add all the flour to the mixture in one go.

4 Beat the mixture vigorously until it comes away from the sides of the saucepan. Leave it to cool for one to two minutes.

5 Beat the eggs in the small bowl. Add them to the mixture a little at a time until it is smooth and shiny.

6 Fit a nozzle* into the piping bag. Put the bag in the measuring jug and fold its top over the sides. Spoon in the mixture.

7 When the bag is full, twist the top to close it. To start piping, squeeze the pastry down through the nozzle.

8 Pipe your shapes on to the greased baking tray and brush them with beaten egg. Bake them for 20 to 25 minutes until golden.

9 Remove the shapes from the oven and prick each one with a cocktail stick. Place the shapes on a wire rack to cool.

* Turn the page to see which nozzle to use to pipe each shape.

Light As Air

You can pipe choux pastry into any shape you like. Follow the instructions at the bottom of the page to make spiders, snakes, worms, puffs and éclairs. When the shapes are cool, fill them with whipped cream and top them with the chocolate icing shown opposite.

You will need

100 g (4 oz) Cooking chocolate

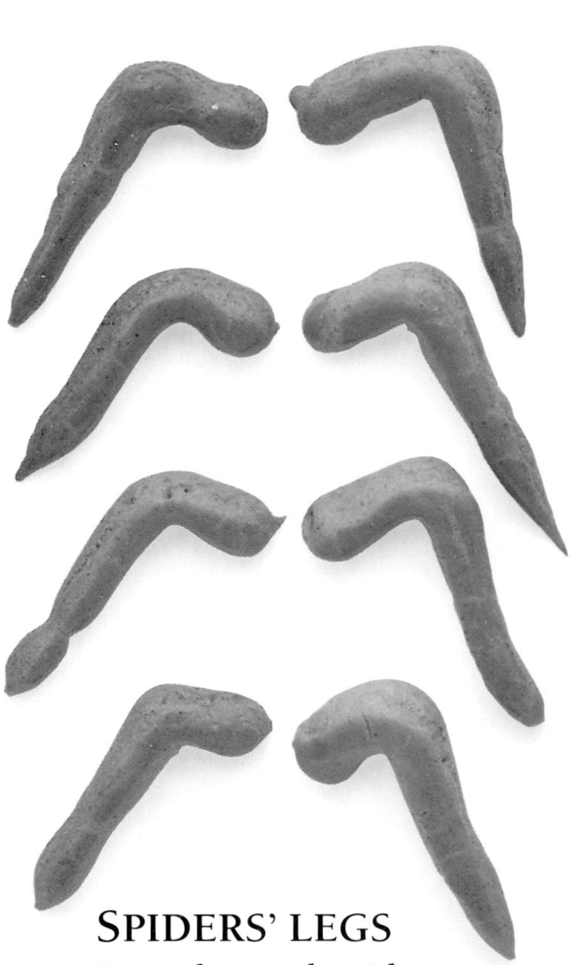

100 g (4 oz) icing sugar

Puffs

To make puffs and spiders' bodies, use the size 8 nozzle and pipe small, round piles on to the baking tray.

Snakes

Use the size 6 nozzle to make the snakes. Start at the head of the snake and pipe a wiggly line for its body.

Spiders' legs

Pipe the spiders' legs using the size 0 nozzle. Make four left legs and four right legs for each spider.

Worms

These are piped with a size 2 nozzle. Pipe the worms as though you are writing commas.

25 g (1 oz) butter

300 ml (1/2 pint) double cream

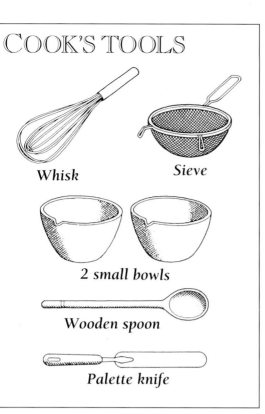

What to do

3 tablespoons water

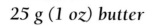

1 Whisk the cream in a small bowl until it is thick and fluffy. Slice the puffs and éclairs in half and spoon the cream into them.

2 Cut the butter and chocolate into pieces. Put them in the saucepan and stir them together over a low heat until they melt.

ECLAIRS

Eclairs are made with the size 8 nozzle. Pipe 5 cm lines of pastry for mini éclairs and 10 cm lines for big ones.

3 Stir in the water. Remove the mixture from the heat. Sift the icing sugar and then add it to the mixture. Stir until smooth.

4 Spread icing along the buns, éclairs and snakes with a palette knife. Dip the worms in the icing with your fingers.

Choux Show

Here are some ideas for decorating your choux shapes. The spider's web was made by piping some of the chocolate icing on to a large white plate. Try piping other animals to make a choux zoo for a special tea or party.

The finished cakes

Currants

Red liquorice

Sugar balls

Sugar strands

SNAKES

The snakes are filled with cream and topped with chocolate icing. Try making a family of snakes, each snake longer than the last.

Currant and cream eyes

Red liquorice forked tongue

Sugar strand markings

58

SPIDERS

To make spiders, cut some puffs in half and fill them with cream. Arrange four legs on each side of the spiders and pipe more cream on top. Add currants for eyes.

WORMS

The worms have been dipped in chocolate icing and then covered in sugar balls before the icing set.

Sugar balls

ECLAIRS

Chocolate éclairs are topped with a thick layer of the chocolate icing and filled with lots of whipped cream.

PUFFS AND PROFITEROLES

Choux puffs can be eaten like little cakes as shown here, or as a delicious dessert, filled with cream and covered in lots of chocolate icing.

Fruit Fools

You can make fruit fools with any fruit soft enough to mash with a fork. Here you can see how to make strawberry or banana fool. The amount of fruit shown for either sort will make four small fools.

You will need

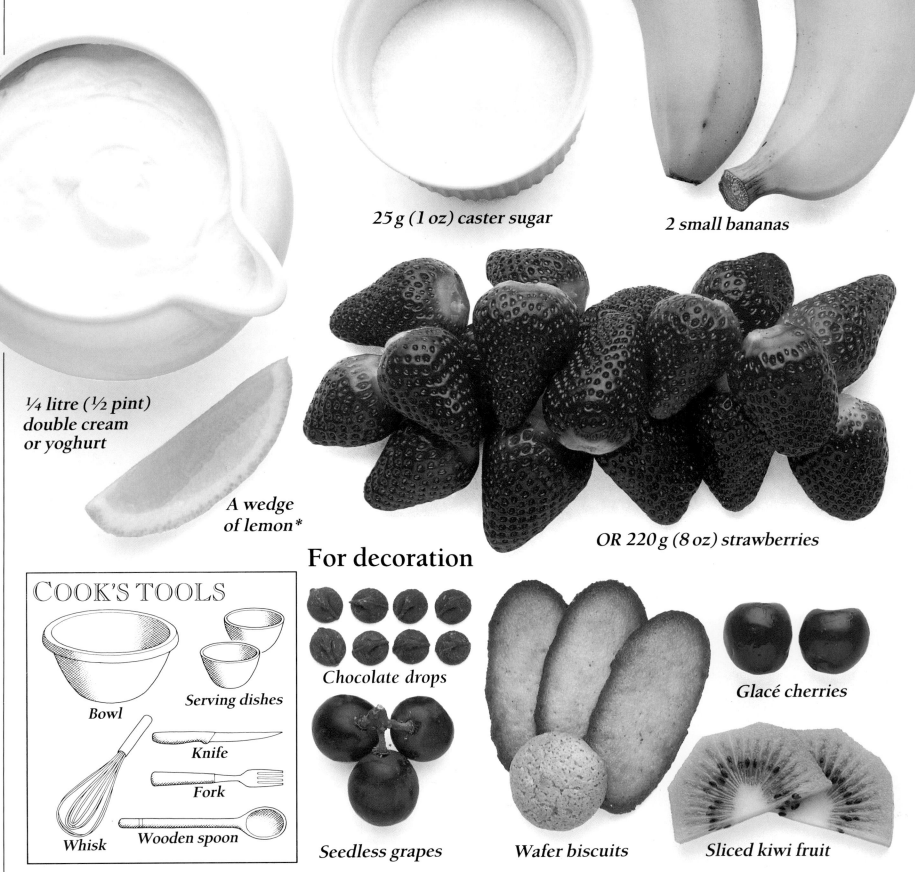

25 g (1 oz) caster sugar

2 small bananas

¼ litre (½ pint) double cream or yoghurt

A wedge of lemon*

OR 220 g (8 oz) strawberries

For decoration

Chocolate drops

Glacé cherries

Seedless grapes

Wafer biscuits

Sliced kiwi fruit

COOK'S TOOLS

Bowl

Serving dishes

Knife

Fork

Whisk

Wooden spoon

*A few drops of lemon juice will stop the banana fool losing its colour.

What you do

1 Cut the strawberries in half or peel and slice the bananas. Put the fruit in the bowl and mash it with a fork until it is smooth.

2 Whisk the cream or yogurt until it is thick and creamy. Add this and the sugar to the mashed fruit. Stir them in well.

3 Pour the fruit mixture into the serving dishes or glasses. Decorate them as shown below, or however you like.

BEAR FOOL

FOOLISH DOG

The banana-fool bear has biscuit ears, eyes made of biscuits and chocolate drops, a cherry nose and a slice of kiwi fruit for a mouth

The strawberry-fool dog has sliced strawberry ears, eyes made of grapes, a biscuit and chocolate-drop nose, and whiskers made of kiwi fruit.

FLOWERING FOOL

The flower pattern on this strawberry fool is made of sliced kiwi fruit and glacé cherries arranged around a grape in the middle.

61

CHOCOLATE DIPS

You can make delicious homemade sweets by dipping your favourite fruits and nuts into melted chocolate. Make sweets out of the things shown below and put them in pretty sweet papers to give away as presents. You can also use them to decorate a special cake, or best of all – just enjoy eating them!

You will need

150 g (6 oz) plain chocolate

Cherries

Mandarin segments

COOK'S TOOLS

Small bowl

Small saucepan

Wooden spoon

Cocktail sticks

Waxed paper

Paper sweet cases

Brazil nuts

Blanched almonds

Walnuts

Melting the chocolate

1 Break the chocolate up into a bowl. Heat some water in the saucepan over a low heat until it just begins to bubble.

2 Stand the bowl over the saucepan over a low heat. Stir the chocolate with a wooden spoon until it completely melts.

3 Turn off the heat. Very carefully move the bowl off the saucepan to a mat or teatowel.

Strawberries

Seedless grapes

Dipping the fruit and nuts

4 One at a time, put a piece of fruit on a cocktail stick and dip half of it into the chocolate. Then put it on to waxed paper to dry.

5 Using your fingers, dip the nuts halfway into the melted chocolate, one at a time. Let them dry on the waxed paper.

Arranging your sweets

You can put the finished sweets in paper sweet cases. If they are for a special occasion, arrange them in circular patterns on a large plate.

Making Meringues

Meringues are deliciously sweet and crunchy and are made from only the whites of eggs, some sugar and a little salt. Separating the egg white from the yolk is quite tricky because yolks break very easily, so always start with more eggs than you need! Be very careful not to allow any yolk to mix with the egg whites, or the recipe won't work.

Meringues take five hours to cook because they have to be baked in a cool oven to keep them white. Start baking in the morning, so that you don't have to stay up all night!

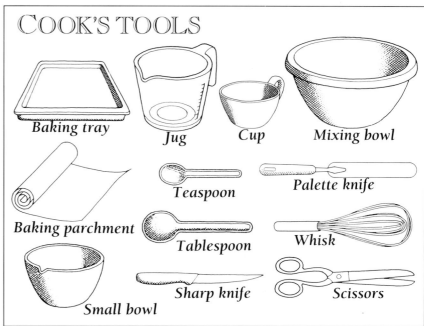

Cook's Tools

Baking tray | Jug | Cup | Mixing bowl

Baking parchment | Teaspoon | Palette knife

Tablespoon | Whisk

Small bowl | Sharp knife | Scissors

You will need

A pinch of salt

2 eggs

Glacé cherries

Currants

100 g (4 oz) caster sugar

Candied orange peel

64

What to do

1 Set oven at its lowest setting. Cut out a square of parchment the same size as the baking tray. Put it on top of the baking tray.

2 *Crack one egg in half and pour the yolk from one half of the shell into the other, letting the egg white fall into the jug.

3 Tip the yolk into the cup and the white into the small bowl. Do the same thing again to separate the second egg.

Nests

4 Add a pinch of salt to the egg whites in the small bowl. Beat the egg whites with the whisk until they form stiff peaks.

5 Whisk the sugar into the egg whites a little at a time, until you have used all the sugar and the meringue looks glossy.

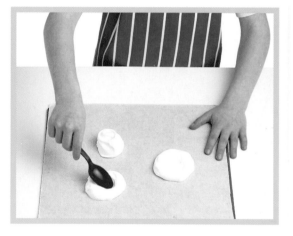

6 Shape a heaped tablespoonful of meringue into a circle on the baking tray. Make a hollow in the middle with a teaspoon.

Ghosts

7 Spread tablespoonfuls of meringue into ghost shapes with a teaspoon. Cut pieces of glacé cherry to make eyes.

Snowmen

8 Use a teaspoonful of meringue for the head and a tablespoonful for the body. Decorate with pieces of currant, candied peel and cherry.

9 Bake the meringue ghosts, snowmen and nests slowly for four to five hours until firm. Put them on a wire rack to cool.

*Ask an adult to help you with this.

Snow-White Surprises

Meringue nests make mouth-watering desserts when they are filled with cream and fruit. Use tinned fruit salad or fresh, soft fruits (like the ones shown here) and arrange them in patterns on the cream-filled nests.

You could make nests at Easter, and fill them with chocolate eggs, or make ghosts for a Hallowe'en treat. Snowmen are great fun as Christmas decorations that you can eat!

Tinned, stoned cherries

Tinned mandarin segments

You will need

Seedless black and green grapes

120 ml (4 fl oz) double cream

Strawberries

Tinned peach chunks

Filling the nests

1 Pour the cream into a small bowl. Whisk the cream until it is thick and fluffy and forms soft peaks.

2 Cut off all the strawberry stalks. Slice some of the strawberries and cut others into quarters with a sharp knife*.

3 Spoon the whipped cream into the nests and arrange the pieces of fruit in pretty patterns on top of them.

66

* Ask an adult to help you.

The finished meringues

MERINGUE NESTS

Slice of strawberry

Piece of strawberry

Black grape

Mandarin segment

Whipped cream

Tinned cherry

Green grape

GHOSTS

Pieces of glacé cherry for eyes

Peach chunk

SNOWMEN

Nose made from a triangle of candied peel

Currant eyes

Slice of glacé cherry for a mouth

Currant buttons

Ice Cream Sundaes

Ice cream sundaes are great fun to make. All you need is ice cream, some sauces and lots of tasty things to put on top. You must make sundaes quite fast, so that they don't melt. Put them in the fridge as you finish them, or eat them at once!

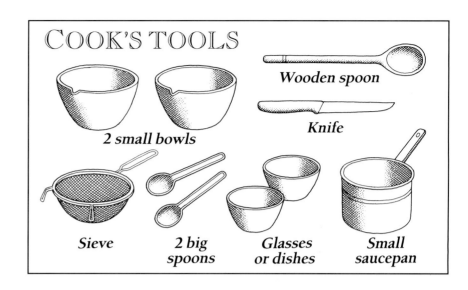

Cook's Tools

2 small bowls

Wooden spoon

Knife

Sieve

2 big spoons

Glasses or dishes

Small saucepan

You will need

Vanilla ice cream

Chocolate ice cream

Strawberry ice cream

For decoration

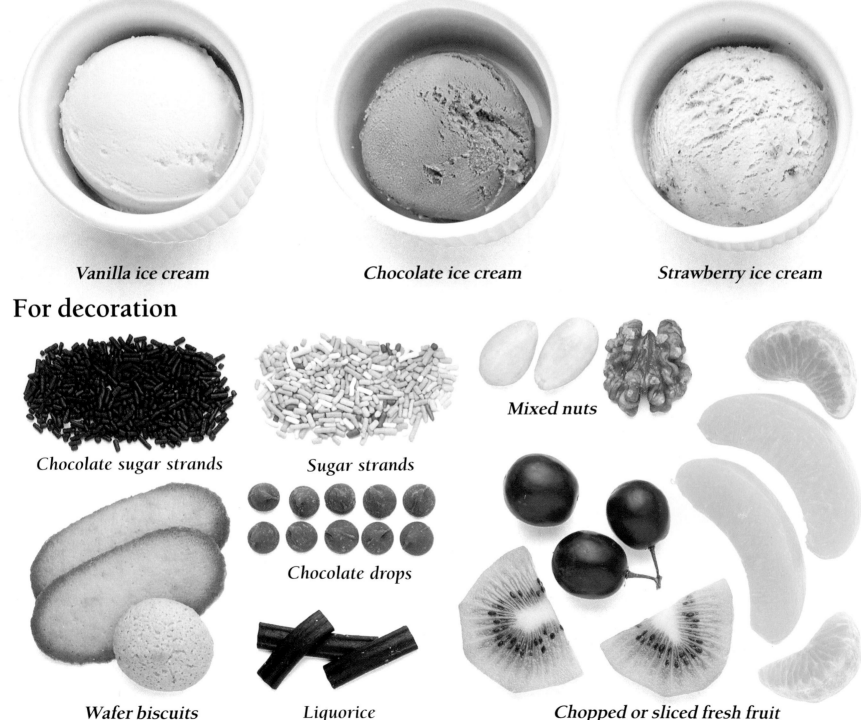

Chocolate sugar strands

Sugar strands

Mixed nuts

Chocolate drops

Wafer biscuits

Liquorice

Chopped or sliced fresh fruit

Making the sauces

For raspberry sauce

150 g (6 oz) raspberries (frozen or fresh)

Raspberry sauce

1 Wash the raspberries and put them in a sieve over a bowl. Then push the raspberries through the sieve using a wooden spoon.

2 Add the caster sugar to the raspberry pulp a little at a time. Then stir the sauce vigorously until all the sugar has dissolved.

Chocolate sauce

1 Break up the chocolate. Put it in the small bowl with the water. Heat some water in the saucepan until it gently bubbles.

2 Place the bowl over the saucepan until the chocolate melts. Turn off the heat and stir the chocolate until smooth.

75 g (3 oz) caster sugar

For chocolate sauce

100 g (4 oz) plain chocolate

3 tablespoons water

Spicy Biscuits

You can make spicy biscuits in all kinds of different shapes. You can make them for parties or just for tea. The ingredients shown here will make about twenty-five biscuits. On the next four pages you can find out how to cut out and decorate your biscuits.

You will need

75 g (3 oz) butter

1 small egg

275 g (10 oz) plain flour

Making the biscuit dough

1 Set the oven at 170°C/325°F/ Gas Mark 3. Sift the flour, baking powder and cinnamon into a mixing bowl. Stir in the sugar.

2 Add the butter and cut it up. Rub the flour mixture and butter together with your fingertips until it looks like breadcrumbs.

3 Break the egg into a jug and beat it with a fork. Add the golden syrup and mix it with the egg until smooth.

70

50 g (2 oz) golden syrup

1 level teaspoon
baking powder

COOK'S TOOLS

Mixing bowl

Wooden spoon

Rolling pin

Measuring jug   Sieve

Biscuit
cutters

Knife

Fork

Palette knife   Greased baking tray

100 g (4oz) soft brown sugar

1 dessertspoon cinnamon

4 Make a hollow in the flour mixture and pour in the egg mixture. Mix everything together until you have a big ball of dough.

5 Put the ball of dough into a plastic bag. Place it in the fridge for 30 minutes, which will make it easier to roll out.

6 Sprinkle some flour on a table and your rolling pin. Roll out the dough evenly until it is about 0.5 cm (¼ in) thick.

Turn the page to see what to do next.

DECORATIVE BISCUIT SHAPES

Cutting out the dough

1 Use biscuit cutters to make different shaped biscuits. To do this, press the cutter down into the dough, then lift the cutter off.

2 With a palette knife, lift each biscuit on to the baking tray. (If they won't all fit, bake the biscuits in two batches.)

3 You can decorate the biscuits now, as shown below. If you want to ice the biscuits, leave them plain when you cook them.

Decorating your biscuits

Look for lots of different cutters to use for your biscuits. You can make biscuits shaped like animals, people, stars and moons, and even dinosaurs. Here are some things you can use to decorate them.

You will need

Glacé cherries

Walnuts

Sesame seeds

Currants

Blanched almonds

Uncooked biscuits

72

Turn the page to find out how to ice biscuits.

Cooking the biscuits

4 Put the baking tray on a high shelf in the oven. Bake the biscuits for 15–20 minutes, until they are golden brown.

5 When cooked, take the biscuits out of the oven and move them on to a wire rack. They will harden as they cool.

Arranging your biscuits

Make a family of biscuit people and line them up, or use a blue plate as a pond for some ducks or as a sky for lots of stars.

Here are the finished biscuits warm from the oven

Easy Icing

To make fancier biscuits you can ice them before decorating them. You must cook the biscuits plain and make sure that they have cooled completely before icing them. Below you can find out how to make white icing and chocolate flavoured icing.

25 g (1 oz) cocoa powder (for chocolate icing only)

You will need

100 g (4 oz) icing sugar

1 tablespoon hot water

Glacé cherries

Making the icing

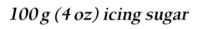

1 Sift the icing sugar into the small bowl. Add the water a little at a time, mixing it with the sugar to make a smooth paste.

2 To make chocolate icing, use 75 g (3 oz) icing sugar and cocoa powder and make it the same way as the white icing.

3 Spoon a little icing on to each biscuit and spread it out evenly with a wet knife. Don't worry if it dribbles down the edges a bit.

Decorating the biscuits

4 Before the icing sets, decorate your biscuits with any of the things shown below. You can make patterns on them, or decorate them to look like faces or animals. Here are some ideas to try.

Chocolate drops

Coloured chocolate sweets

Chocolate sugar strands

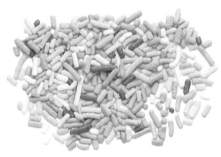

Sugar strands

PEANUT BUTTER COOKIES

These mouth-watering cookies are very quick and easy to make. Crunchy peanut butter makes the cookies very nutty, but use smooth peanut butter if you prefer it. Bake the cookies for 15 minutes if you like them soft in the middle, or for 20 to 25 minutes if you like them crisp. Store the cookies in an airtight tin to keep them fresh.

You will need

175 g (6 oz) soft
brown sugar

1 egg

125 g (4 oz) crunchy peanut butter

125 g (4 oz) soft butter

175 g (6 oz)
self-raising flour

COOK'S TOOLS

2 teaspoons

Wooden spoon

Mixing
bowl

Wire rack

Knife   Greased baking tray

What to do

1 Set the oven to 350°F/180°C/ Gas Mark 4. Cut up the butter in the bowl and add the sugar. Beat them together until fluffy.

2 Add the peanut butter, flour and egg and beat everything together with the wooden spoon until the mixture is smooth.

3 Put teaspoonfuls of mixture on to a baking tray. Bake the cookies for 15 to 25 minutes*. Then put them on a wire rack, to cool.

The finished cookies

* See the introduction to this recipe.

CHOCOLATE BROWNIES

Chocolate brownies are a great American treat. They are crisp on the outside, but wonderfully soft and chewy inside. Below are all the ingredients you need to make dark chocolate and walnut brownies. On the next page you will find the finished brownie squares.

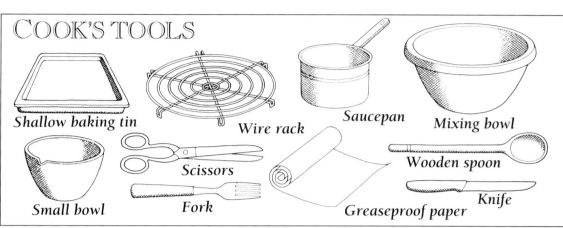
You will need

65 g (2½ oz) butter

50 g (2 oz) plain chocolate

What to do

1 Set the oven to 180°C/350°F/ Gas Mark 4. Cut a square of greaseproof paper and put it in the bottom of the greased baking tin.

2 Heat some water in the saucepan until it just starts to bubble. Put the butter in the small bowl and cut it up.

3 Break up the chocolate into the bowl and stand it over the pan. Stir the butter and chocolate together until they have melted.

78

65 g (2¹/₂ oz) walnut pieces

*175 g (6 oz)
soft brown sugar*

2 eggs

*65 g (2 oz)
self-raising flour*

4 Break the eggs into the mixing bowl and beat with a fork. Add the flour, walnuts and sugar and mix with the wooden spoon.

5 Pour the melted chocolate and butter into the mixture in the bowl and beat them hard until the mixture is smooth.

6 Pour the mixture into the baking tin and bake for 30 to 35 minutes. Leave it to cool in the tin and then cut it into squares.

A Brownie Pack

Brownies can be made with any kind of chocolate or nut. Try using white or milk chocolate instead of dark chocolate and using other sorts of nut, such as hazelnuts, peanuts or almonds instead of walnuts.

The finished brownies